The True Story of Jesus

Rashid Ahmad Chaudhry

The True Story of Jesus

ISLAM INTERNATIONAL PUBLICATIONS LTD.

The True Story of Jesus[as]
Written by Rashid Ahmad Chaudhry

First edition (*The Story of Jesus*) in the UK, 1979
Second edition, 1981
Third edition: 1997
Fourth edition (ISBN: 1 85372 625 7), 2003
Fifth edition published in India, 2017
Reprinted in UK, 2018

© Islam International Publications Ltd.

Published by
Islam International Publications Ltd.
Unit 3, Bourne Mill Business Park
Guildford Road
Farnham, Surrey GU9 9PS, UK

Printed in UK at
Raqeem Press
Farnham, Surrey GU9 9PS

For further information please visit www.alislam.org.

Cover design by: Usman Nasir Choudhary

ISBN 978-1-84880-025-0
11 10 9 8 7 6 5 4 3 2

Contents

Foreword .... *v*

Chapter One—Historical Background 1
Chapter Two—Glad Tidings of a Son to Mary 7
Chapter Three—Early Life of Jesus 15
Chapter Four—Jesus as a Prophet of God 19
Chapter Five—The Teachings of Jesus 23
Chapter Six—Miracles of Jesus 31
Chapter Seven—Enemies Plan to Kill Jesus 37
Chapter Eight—Trial of Jesus 47
Chapter Nine—Jesus is Hung on the Cross 55
Chapter Ten—Chronology of Jesus' Trial 67
Chapter Eleven—Jesus Migrates to Other
 Countries 77
Chapter Twelve—The Shroud of Turin 95
Chapter Thirteen—The Second Advent of Jesus .. 99

Names of Prophets *109*
Publisher's Note *111*
Glossary *113*

Foreword

Jesus, son of Mary, peace be upon him, stands out as one of the most controversial characters in religious history. Differing opinions about him have drawn divisive lines between billions of people, and millions have killed or cured in his name. The Jews, Christians, and Muslims all hold different views regarding Jesus' birth, mission, miracles, and death.

Jews believe that Jesus was a false prophet because he died an accursed death on the cross. Christians, on the other hand, agree with the Jews that Jesus died on the cross, but claim it was only to carry the curse of the entire world's sins. They believe that Jesus is God and willingly sacrificed his life on the cross to pay the penalty of all mankind's sins; he was resurrected on the third day and ascended to Heaven.

In contrast to both of these viewpoints, all Muslims believe that Jesus[as] was a truthful prophet of God, but he was certainly not God Himself. Most Muslims do not believe that Jesus was even hung on the cross. They believe that someone who resembled Jesus was crucified in his stead, while Jesus was lifted bodily to Heaven where he is still waiting to come back to earth in the Latter Days.

Ahmadi Muslims contend that Jesus[as] was, in fact, hung on the cross, but did not die upon it. In this way Ahmadi Muslims honour Jesus[as] as a true prophet of God by proving that he was not accursed. He was unconscious when taken down from the cross and was placed in the sepulchre (a spacious tomb) where a potent ointment was applied to heal his wounds. Having recovered from his wounds, he travelled to other countries where many of his people, the Israelites, had settled. These far away Israelite tribes were known as the Lost Sheep of the House of Israel. Finally, Jesus[as] reached Kashmir where he eventually passed away after preaching the *Injil* [the Gospel] to the Israelites. In fact, there is a tomb in Kashmir which is believed to be the tomb of Jesus[as].

The *True Story of Jesus*[as] is a book that was originally prepared by the members of the Children's Book Committee. This Committee was appointed by Hazrat Khalifatul-Masih IV[rta] and worked under his direct supervision and guidance. May the Benevolent Lord bless their efforts and sacrifices in His cause.

I would also like to express my gratitude to Maulana Ata-ul-Mujeeb Rashed, Imam of the London Mosque, for his efforts in reviewing the original publication, and to Ayesha Noor, Faraz Hussain, Khalil Malik, Naser-ud-Din Shams, and Abdul-Wahab Mirza for reviewing the current manuscript and providing valuable suggestions. May Almighty Allah bless them and their families for their respective contributions.

Finally, it is my sincere hope and prayer that this booklet become a source of enlightenment welcomed by children, teachers, and parents alike. O Allah, let it be so.

Munir-ud-Din Shams
Additional Wakilut-Tasneef
London, January 2017

Chapter One— Historical Background

On the edge of the Roman Empire there was a small country, Palestine. The Romans had conquered Palestine in the year 63 BC. In the northern part of this country, in a small hilly town called Nazareth, lived a little girl named Mary. Her father's name was Imran and her mother's name was Hannah. Hannah had made a vow before the birth of the child that she would dedicate her child's life to the service of the Jewish Temple. She had hoped and prayed to give birth to a male child because in those days only male children were accepted in the service of the Temple. But when Mary was born instead, Hannah was perplexed and expressed her anguish to God saying, 'My Lord! I have given birth to a girl.'[1] The Holy Quran states that Allah knew best what she had given birth to.

This implied that the girl, Mary, was not an ordinary girl;

---

1. Holy Quran 3:37

rather, God had bestowed on her those qualities which made her a very special and extraordinary child, even better than the boy Hannah was hoping for. Mary was admitted to the service of God in the Jewish Temple as an exceptional case. The Temple was headed by Zachariah[as], the High Priest, who according to the Holy Quran, was also a Prophet of God. Thus, according to God's design, Mary was brought up under Zachariah's holy and benign care. It is reported that right from her childhood she spent most of her time in her chamber in the remembrance of God. Whenever Zachariah[as] visited her, he found her with provisions. The gifts were evidently brought by visitors to the Temple. Moreover, God had granted her not only material things but also had given her such wisdom that even at an early age she could interpret the Scriptures and answer complex questions in such a manner which were far beyond her age. This surprised Zachariah[as] and addressing her he said, 'O Mary! From where did you attain this?' She replied, 'It is from Allah.' Surely, Allah gives His bounties to whomsoever He pleases without measure.[1]

This pious reply of Mary made a deep impression on the mind of Zachariah[as] and he prayed to God Almighty that he may also be blessed with a child as pious as Mary. Though he was very old and his wife was barren meaning that she was unable to bear a child, yet having full trust in Allah's Omnipotence, he prayed to God:

---

1. Holy Quran 3:38

'My Lord, my bones have indeed become feeble and the hair on my head have turned white like flames, but never, my Lord, have I been unblessed in my prayer to You. And I fear my relations after me, and my wife is barren. Grant me, therefore, a successor from Yourself that he may be heir to me and the House of Jacob. And make him, my Lord, well-pleasing to You.' God replied, 'O Zachariah, We give you glad tidings of a son whose name shall be Yahya, a name We have not given to anyone before.'[1]

Thus, Yahya[as] was born according to Allah's promise and God made him a Prophet to the Israelites. Yahya[as] or John the Baptist, as he is generally known in the Christian world, also happened to be a forerunner of Jesus[as], in fulfilment of the prophecy mentioned in the Old Testament, which states: 'Behold, I will send you Elijah the Prophet before the coming of the great and dreadful day of the Lord.'[2]

The Jews believed that Prophet Elijah[as] had ascended to Heaven bodily and would descend before the coming of the Messiah. The fact was that Elijah[as] was never taken up to Heaven bodily and therefore could not have descended from Heaven. The Biblical prophecy was fulfilled in the person of John[as] the Baptist, who came in the spirit of Elijah[as].

---

1. Holy Quran 19:5–8
2. Malachi 4:5

Study Questions

QUESTION 1: What was the name of Mary's father?

YOUR RESPONSE: _____

QUESTION 2: What was the name of Mary's mother?

YOUR RESPONSE: _____

QUESTION 3: Why was Hannah upset at the birth of Mary?

YOUR RESPONSE: _____
_____
_____

QUESTION 4: Who was the High Priest at the Temple?

YOUR RESPONSE: _____
_____
_____

QUESTION 5: What did Zachariah[as] find when he used to visit Mary's chamber?

YOUR RESPONSE:
_____
_____
_____
_____

QUESTION 6: What was Zachariah's prayer?

YOUR RESPONSE:
_____
_____
_____
_____

QUESTION 7: What was the name of the son born to him?

YOUR RESPONSE: _____

QUESTION 8: What did Jews believe about Elijah[as]?

YOUR RESPONSE:
_____
_____
_____
_____
_____

QUESTION 9: Who came as a forerunner of Jesus[as]? Explain your answer.

YOUR RESPONSE: _____
_____
_____

Chapter Two—
Glad Tidings of a Son to Mary

Time went by and Mary grew up into a devoted, chaste and truthful woman. One day, while she was praying to God Almighty in seclusion, an angel, in the form of a very handsome man, appeared to her and conveyed the divine message that she would have a son. The vision was so lifelike that Mary, being a virtuous woman, was taken aback as she was under the impression that a young man was really standing before her. Therefore, she said, 'I seek refuge with the Gracious God from you if indeed you fear Him.' The angel replied, 'I am only a messenger from your Lord, that I may bestow a righteous son on you.'[1] This shocked Mary as she was a virgin. She said:

> How can I have a son when no man has touched me, neither have I been unchaste?' The angel said, 'Thus it is, but

---

1. Holy Quran 19:20

your Lord says, 'It is easy for Me; and We shall do so that we may make him a Sign unto people and a mercy from Us, and it is a matter decreed'.[1]

Thus, Mary conceived the child without the agency of a male.

Angels appeared to Mary in her dreams yet again, and gave her the glad tidings of a son who would be called the Messiah, Jesus[as] son of Mary. She was told that he would be honoured in this world and in the next and would be granted nearness to God.

The Birth of Jesus[as]

In order to avoid the scandalous talk of people, she left the town and went to the hills around Bethlehem, the place where Jesus[as] is said to have been born. The town of Bethlehem is about 70 miles from Nazareth and is situated at a height of about two thousand feet above sea level and is surrounded by fertile valleys. There were springs on the hills from which the town got its water supply. Palm trees grew in abundance. It was in this area that Mary stayed for the delivery of her child. It was now summer and there were ripe dates on the palm trees. It is stated in the Gospel of Luke that shepherds were out in the fields, keeping watch through the night over their flock.

As the time of Jesus' birth approached, Mary took rest under a palm tree, which was on the slope of a hill outside Bethlehem. In

---

1. Holy Quran 19:21–22

CHAPTER TWO—GLAD TIDINGS OF A SON TO MARY

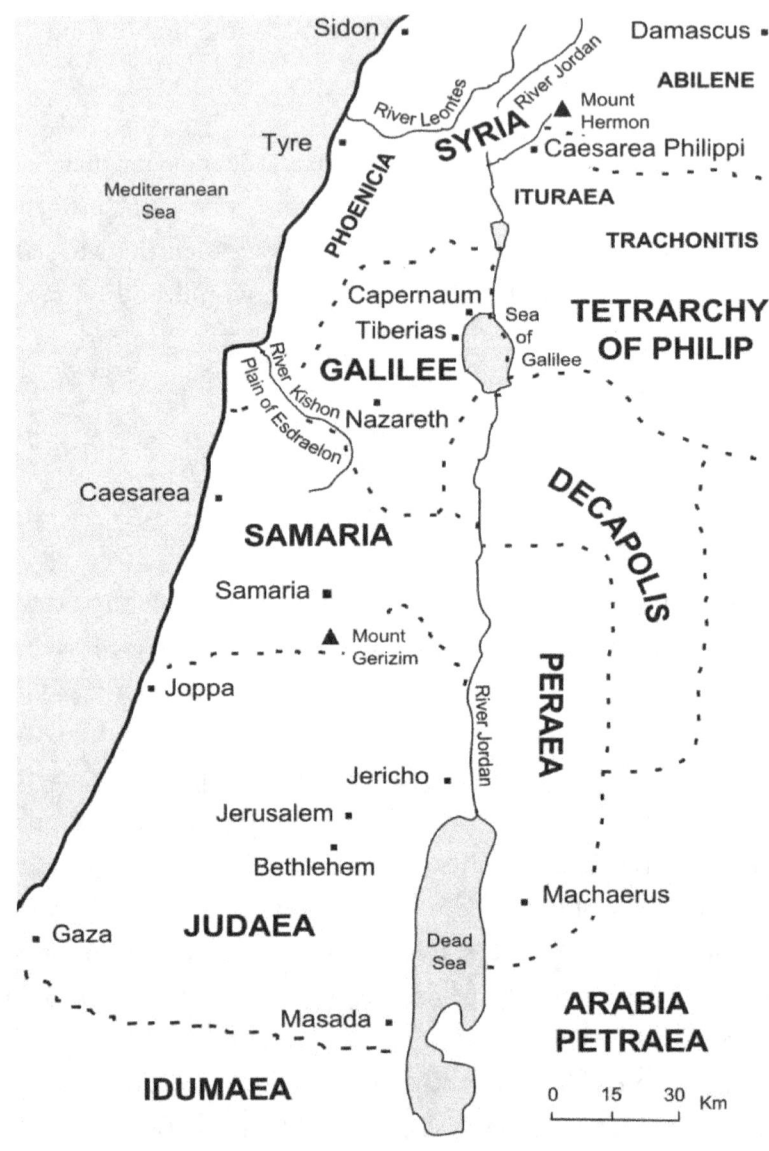

Palestine in the time of Jesus[as]

this sheltered place she gave birth to Jesus[as]. As she went through the pains of childbirth, she exclaimed in agony, 'Would that I had died before this and had become a thing quite forgotten!' At that moment she heard a voice from the side of the slope of the mountain. It was an angel who comforted her saying that she should not grieve. She was told that her Lord has provided a stream underneath her, wherein she may wash herself and the child. The angel said:

> And shake the trunk of the palm tree towards you; it will drop fresh ripe dates upon you. So eat and drink and be at rest. And if you see anyone approaching, say, 'I have vowed a fast to the Gracious God; I will therefore not speak this day to any human being.'[1]

The birth of Jesus[as] was extraordinary in the sense that he was born without the agency of a male. It was miraculous but not contrary to the laws of nature. This unusual form of birth was a warning to the Israelites that their misdeeds had brought an end to their spiritual progeny and that they would no longer be worthy of fathering the Prophets of God. This in fact was a sign to show that the spiritual blessings would be transferred from the progeny of Isaac[as] to that of his brother Ishmael[as], in accordance with God's great prophecy and His covenant with Abraham[as]. Jesus[as] would be the last Israelite Prophet. Muhammad[saw], the Prophet of Islam, came after Jesus[as] in the year 570 AD, and was a descendant of Ishmael[as].

---

1. Holy Quran 19:24–27

Heavenly Sign to Mark the Birth of Jesus[as]

It is stated in the Bible that soon after the birth of Jesus[as] some wise men came from the east to Jerusalem and asked, 'Where is he that is born King of Jews? for we have seen his star in the east.'[1]

This account, if it is true, tells us that a special star, known as the 'Star of Bethlehem' appeared in the sky to mark the birth of a very special child who was to spiritually lead the Israelites. The people, who had the knowledge of stars, might have recognised the star and known that such a child had been born.

This indeed was an extraordinary sign, but we know from the history of religion that God sometimes shows heavenly signs to inform people of great religious events. For example, in present times the eclipses of the sun and the moon occurred in 1894 within the same month of Ramadan according to the prophecy of the Prophet of Islam, to mark the advent of the Mahdi.

It is also related in the Bible that the star guided those wise men to the place where Jesus[as] was born. This seems to be an exaggeration. We know from our own experience that heavenly bodies like stars and the moon cannot lead us to a particular place. They seem to move along with us wherever we go. Again the Bible says that the men came and worshipped Jesus. This cannot be a true account either. Mary, the mother of Jesus, was a pious lady. She believed in one God and worshipped Him alone. Therefore, she could not have allowed anyone to worship her child.

In spite of the fact that the Jews were waiting for the Messiah to

---

1. Matthew 2:2

appear, they rejected Jesus[as]. They believed that the 'King of Israel' would come and lead them to victory over the Romans. They were expecting a mighty king who would come with power and glory. Therefore, when Jesus[as], who was of humble origin, claimed to be the Messiah, he was rejected outright. The Jews were indeed mistaken. Jesus[as] did not claim to be a worldly king. He explained that his kingdom had nothing to do with this physical world.

Study Questions

QUESTION 1: What did Mary say to the angel who appeared to her and what was the reply of the angel?

YOUR RESPONSE:

QUESTION 2: Where was Jesus[as] born?

YOUR RESPONSE:

QUESTION 3: How far is Bethlehem from Nazareth?

YOUR RESPONSE:

CHAPTER TWO—GLAD TIDINGS OF A SON TO MARY

QUESTION 4: Why did Mary leave Nazareth?

YOUR RESPONSE: _____
_____
_____

QUESTION 5: What time of the year was it when Jesus[as] was born?

YOUR RESPONSE: _____

QUESTION 6: Why do we call the birth of Jesus[as] extraordinary?

YOUR RESPONSE: _____
_____
_____
_____
_____
_____

QUESTION 7: Which of the sons of Prophet Abraham[as], had the honour of being the forefather of Prophet Muhammad[saw]?

YOUR RESPONSE: _____
_____

QUESTION 8: Why did the Jews reject Jesus[as]?

YOUR RESPONSE: _____

_____

_____

_____

QUESTION 9: Comment on the Biblical story that the star guided the wise men to the place where Jesus[as] was born.

YOUR RESPONSE: _____

_____

_____

_____

_____

QUESTION 10: Comment on the Biblical story that the wise men worshipped baby Jesus[as].

YOUR RESPONSE: _____

_____

_____

_____

Chapter Three—
Early Life of Jesus

Jesus[as] was an intelligent child. He was obedient and dutiful to his mother and was very kind to every one. Being a specially blessed child, he spoke words of wisdom from his early childhood. Whenever he was confronted with difficult and complex questions, his answers were so profound and wonderful as would not be expected.

Jesus[as] was merely a child when Mary decided to go back to her people. They were riding a donkey when they entered the town. When people learnt of their return they came out of their houses and surrounded Mary. They began to ridicule and taunt her and behaved mischievously towards her. They thought she had committed a sin and censured her by saying, 'O Mary, surely you have committed a monstrous thing. Your father was not a wicked man, nor was your mother an unchaste woman!'[1]

---

1. Holy Quran 19:28–29

There were many a rude remark from the people. Mary was deeply hurt but she did not say anything in reply. Instead she pointed towards Jesus[as] meaning that such a blessed child who was already showing signs of being in communion with God, could not have been the fruit of sin.

At this they said, 'How can we talk to one who is merely a child in the cradle?'; meaning that the boy was too young to give them a meaningful explanation.

Jesus[as] told them, 'I am a servant of Allah. He has given me the Book and has made me a Prophet; and He has made me blessed wheresoever I may be, and has enjoined upon me Prayer and almsgiving so long as I live; and has made me dutiful towards my mother, and has not made me arrogant and graceless.'[1]

People were amazed to listen to such talk. It seemed that God had already informed Jesus[as], perhaps in his dreams, of the spiritual heights he was to climb. Many children because of their love of God are shown such signs. We read another example of such a case in the Holy Quran. Joseph[as], son of Jacob[as], when he was yet a small child, was also shown such dreams regarding the high spiritual status he would achieve in the future.

After listening to Jesus[as] some of the people were very impressed and stopped bothering Mary, while others thought that Mary had put all this into the child's mind which he was just repeating in parrot-like fashion.

Jesus[as] lived in Nazareth, a small secluded town amongst the hills of Galilee, the land of pastures, olive groves and vineyards. There is a veil of obscurity over the period from his childhood to

---

1. Holy Quran 19:30–33

the time he was raised as a Prophet. We do not know much about this period of his life.

Study Questions

QUESTION 1: Why did people ridicule Mary when she returned with the child Jesus[as] to Nazareth?

YOUR RESPONSE: _____
_____
_____

QUESTION 2: What was Mary's response to the accusations?

YOUR RESPONSE: _____
_____
_____
_____

QUESTION 3: What did baby Jesus[as] say to the people?

YOUR RESPONSE: _____
_____
_____
_____

Chapter Four— Jesus as a Prophet of God

Throughout religious history, we find that over time the followers of every religion deviate gradually from the true path and begin to wander in the wilderness of sin. The Jewish people were no exception. By the time of the advent of Jesus[as] they had virtually become spiritually dead. They were corrupt and used to indulge in evil practices of all sorts. They were arrogant and very hard-hearted. One of their malpractices was that they interpolated the teachings of Judaism and twisted the laws of the Torah to their own advantage. They had indeed ceased to act upon the teachings of the Torah. They also believed that they were the favourites of Allah and therefore immune from any punishment. It is to these people that Jesus[as] was sent as a Messenger of God, the Messiah they were waiting for. The task assigned to Jesus[as] was to transform them once again into kind-hearted people and bring them back to God.

When Jesus[as] started his divine mission and tried to deliver the message of God, the Jews did not listen to him and rejected him outright claiming that he was an impostor. Jesus[as] explained the true spirit of the Torah, and tried to remove the misunderstandings about the Law, but the Jews did not accept his explanations. On the contrary, they charged him with abrogating the laws of the Torah.

In reply to these accusations Jesus[as] told them:

> Think not that I am come to destroy the Law and the Prophets: I am not come to destroy, but to fulfil. For verily I say unto you, Until the heaven and earth pass, one jot or one tittle shall in no way pass from the Law, until all be fulfilled. Whosoever therefore shall break one of these least commandments, and shall teach men so, he shall be called the least in the Kingdom of Heaven: but whosoever shall do and teach them, the same shall be called great in the Kingdom of Heaven. For I say unto you, That except your righteousness shall exceed the righteousness of the scribes and Pharisees, you shall in no case enter into the Kingdom of Heaven.[1]

But the clergy among the Jews turned a deaf ear to his admonitions. The Jews also accused him of blasphemy, saying that he had claimed to be God. Jesus[as] tried to convince them that they were mistaken and in no way had he claimed to be God, but they were adamant and wanted to put him to death, as death was the punishment of blasphemy according to Jewish laws.

---

1. Matthew 5:17–20

The Jewish divines also accused Jesus[as] for not believing in the prophecy mentioned in the Scriptures about the second coming of Elijah[as]. They believed that Elijah[as] had gone to Heaven bodily, as the Scripture stated, 'There appeared a chariot of fire, and horses of fire, and parted them…and Elijah went up by a whirlwind into heaven.'[1]

It is also stated, 'Behold! I will send you Elijah the prophet before the coming of the great and dreadful day of the Lord.'[2]

They therefore believed that Elijah[as] would descend bodily from Heaven before the advent of the Messiah, hence they used to taunt the followers of Jesus[as] by saying, 'Where is Elijah? How can Jesus claim to be the Messiah when we haven't seen Elijah yet descending from the sky?' Once, when his disciples told him that the Jewish clergy mockingly inquire of them about the descent of Elijah[as], Jesus[as] said, 'I tell you that Elijah has already come, and people did not recognise him, but treated him just as they pleased. So also the son of man will suffer at their hands. Then the disciples understood that he was speaking to them about John the Baptist.'[3]

Jesus[as], being guided by God, understood this prophecy correctly. He knew that Elijah[as] was never taken up to Heaven bodily and therefore would not descend bodily from Heaven. He seems to have been informed by God that the prophecy was fulfilled in the person of John[as] the Baptist; and by the second coming of Elijah[as], it was meant that a person would come in the spirit and power of Elijah[as]. Jesus[as] understood that such prophecies were

---

1. II Kings 2:11
2. Malachi 4:5
3. Matthew 17:12–13

metaphoric and should not be taken literally. The Jews, however, refused to accept his explanation. They said that Jesus[as] was an impostor who attributed things to God which God had never said. Thus, they became the sworn enemies of Jesus[as] and began to persecute him and his followers as much as they could.

Study Questions

QUESTION 1: Why did the Jews taunt the followers of Jesus[as]?

YOUR RESPONSE:

QUESTION 2: What were the Jewish beliefs about the prophecy of the second coming of Elijah[as]?

YOUR RESPONSE:

QUESTION 3: How did Jesus[as] interpret the prophecy?

YOUR RESPONSE:

Chapter Five—
The Teachings of Jesus

Christians believe that the Godhead is made up of three distinct persons: God, the Father; God, the son; and God, the Holy Ghost. They call this the Trinity. The fact is that Jesus[as] did not believe in the concept of Trinity. This doctrine is not taught anywhere in the New Testament or in the Old Testament before it. The entire concept of Trinity was foreign to the thinking of Jesus[as] and to the early Christians. The early Christians believed Jesus[as] to be someone who was sent by God. The term *Trinity*, therefore, was concocted after the Crucifixion. As far as Jesus[as] was concerned, he never commanded any person to worship him nor did he ever claim to be God. We cannot find a single reference in the New Testament where he had referred to himself as God or implied that he was God nor instructed people to worship him as God. On the contrary, we find that he believed in the absolute Oneness of God and he called his followers to worship the one True God.

We find that the expression 'Lord' was used for him in the

Bible but there is no evidence that those who made use of this expression with reference to him believed or meant to convey that he was God. It was used as a synonym for *master*. Jesus[as] taught people to worship God, the only Lord. When asked 'Which is the first commandment of all?' Jesus[as] replied, 'The first of all commandments is, 'Hear, O Israel; The Lord our God is one Lord: And you shall love the Lord your God with all your heart, and with all your soul, and with all your mind, and with all your strength.' The second is, 'Love your neighbour as you love yourself.' There is no other commandment greater than these.'[1]

As for himself, he always looked upon himself as human. According to the Holy Quran he stated, 'I come to you with a Sign from your Lord.'[2]

It is clear therefore that he was only a Messenger of Allah. The New Testament also confirmed this. Jesus[as] is reported to have said, 'I have not spoken on my own authority, but the Father who sent me has commanded me what I must say and speak.'[3] He also says, 'My doctrine is not mine, but His who sent me.'[4] On another occasion he said, 'I came down from heaven, not to do not my own will, but the will of Him who sent me.'[5]

Thus, it is clear that he regarded himself as a Messenger of God and not God or the literal son of God.

---

1. Mark 12:28–31
2. Holy Quran 3:50
3. John 12:49
4. John 7:16
5. John 6:38

The Holy Quran Refutes Trinity

The Holy Quran states:

> O People of the Book! Exceed not the limits in your religion, and say not of Allah anything but the truth. Verily, the Messiah, Jesus, son of Mary, was only a Messenger of God and a fulfilment of His Word which He sent down to Mary, and a mercy from Him. So believe in Allah and His Messengers, and say not, 'They are three'. Desist, it will be better for you. Verily, Allah is the only One God. Far is it from His Holiness that He should have a son. To Him belongs whatever is in the heavens and whatever is in the earth, and sufficient is Allah as a Guardian.[1]

At another place it states:

> And when Allah will say, 'O Jesus, son of Mary, did you say to men, 'Take me and my mother for two gods beside Allah'?', he will answer, 'Holy are You. I could never say that to which I had no right. If I had said it, You would have surely known it. You know what is in my mind, but I know not what is in Your mind. It is only You who are the Knower of hidden things.
>
> I said nothing to them except that which You commanded me: 'Worship Allah, my Lord and your Lord.'

---

1. Holy Quran 4:172

And I was a witness over them as long as I remained among them, but since You caused me to die, You have been the Watcher over them; and You are Witness over all things. If You punish them, they are Your servants; and if You forgive them, You surely are the Mighty, the Wise.[1]

It is evident from the above verses that Jesus[as], when he will be questioned by God on the Day of Judgement, will declare that he did not tell his people to worship anyone but God. The verses also prove that Jesus[as] had died like any other human being.

The Term 'Son Of God'

The term 'son of God' used for Jesus[as] in the New Testament should not be taken literally; rather, it was used metaphorically to mean someone who is a beloved of God and the one who has a close relationship with Him. In fact, the same title has been used in the Old Testament for earlier Prophets. For example, it is written that 'Israel is My son, even My firstborn.'[2]

At another place in the Old Testament, it is written that God said about David[as], 'I will make him My firstborn, higher than the kings of the earth.'[3] Similarly, God said about Solomon[as], 'He shall be My son, and I will be his Father.'[4]

---

1. Holy Quran 5:117–119
2. Exodus 4:22
3. Psalms 89:27
4. I Chronicles 22:10

When we read the New Testament we find that people are metaphorically described as *children of God*. It says: 'That you may be the children of your Father which is in Heaven.'[1]

The Holy Quran denounces the Christian dogma that Jesus[as] is the literal son of God. It says;

> And they say, 'The Gracious God has taken unto Himself a son.' Assuredly, you have indeed uttered a most hideous thing. The heavens might well-nigh burst thereat, and the earth cleave asunder, and the mountains fall down in pieces. Because they ascribe a son to the Gracious God. It becomes not the Gracious God that He should take unto Himself a son.[2]

Jesus' Advice to his Disciples

As is the case with every Prophet of God, Jesus[as] was opposed in his mission. People tried to put an end to his message, but in spite of all this, the number of his admirers continued to grow gradually. People came from far and wide to ask for his blessings. The first to become his disciples were poor people like fishermen. Soon he had a number of followers who helped him in delivering the divine message to the Israelites.

He told his disciples that they should acquire their earnings lawfully and honestly and that their earnings should also be spent

---

1. Matthew 5:45
2. Holy Quran 19:89–93

in the service of the needy and the poor. He taught them meekness and humility. He laid great stress on mercy and forgiveness. Jesus[as] exhorted them to convey the message of God even in the face of all opposition with courage and determination. He told them that they could not succeed unless they were prepared to sacrifice their honour and wealth in the cause of Allah, and give up their personal comfort for the sake of Allah. He is reported to have said:

> Lay not up for yourselves treasures upon earth, where moth and rust corrupt, and where thieves break through and steal: But lay up for yourselves treasures in heaven, where neither moth nor rust corrupt, and where thieves do not break through nor steal: 'For where your treasure is, there will your heart be also.'[1]

He warned them of the persecutions they were to face in the name of religion. He said:

> Blessed are you when people shall revile you, and persecute you, and shall say all manner of evil against you falsely, for my sake. Rejoice, and be exceeding glad: for great is your reward in heaven.[2]

The followers of Jesus[as] suffered greatly at the hands of the Jews but remained steadfast. Indeed, they had to make many sacrifices

---

1. Matthew 6:19–21
2. Matthew 5:11–12

for their beliefs, which they did willingly. They were sincere helpers in the cause of Allah, believing in the mission of Jesus[as] and making no secret of their faith. But there were some who were weak-hearted. The Bible describes some disciples in particular who showed weakness in their faith at the time of trial.

As Jesus[as] was sent specifically to the Israelites, he expressly instructed his disciples not to preach to anyone but the Israelites. He is reported to have said, 'Go not into the way of the Gentiles, and into any city of the Samaritans enter ye not: But go rather to the lost sheep of the house of Israel [i.e., the Israelites]. And as you go, preach, saying, 'The kingdom of heaven is at hand.'[1]

Study Questions

QUESTION 1: What do Christians mean by the Trinity?

YOUR RESPONSE:

---

1. Matthew 10:5–7

QUESTION 2: Is there any mention of Trinity in the Bible?

YOUR RESPONSE: _____

QUESTION 3: Give two reasons to prove that Jesus[as] was not God.

YOUR RESPONSE: _____
_____
_____

QUESTION 4: What does the title 'son of God' mean? Explain by giving examples from the Bible.

YOUR RESPONSE: _____
_____
_____
_____

QUESTION 5: What does the Holy Quran say about the Christian dogma that Jesus[as] was 'son of God'?

YOUR RESPONSE: _____
_____
_____
_____

Chapter Six— Miracles of Jesus

It was the habit of Jesus[as] to talk in parables, a way of talking which was predicted in the previous scriptures to be a characteristic of his speech. Jesus[as] showed miracles to his people just like other Prophets of God showed miracles to their people.

The Holy Quran tells us some of the miracles performed by Jesus[as]. It says that Allah had sent Jesus[as] as a Messenger to the Children of Israel with this message:

> I come to you with a Sign from your Lord, which is, that I will fashion out for you a creation out of clay after the manner of a bird, then I will breathe into it a new spirit and it will become a soaring being by the command of Allah; and I will heal the night blind and the leprous, and I will give life to the dead, by the command of Allah.[1]

---

1. Holy Quran 3:50

This does not mean that Jesus[as] literally created some birds or gave life to some people who were dead, because such a belief is totally opposed to Quranic teachings. The Holy Quran tells us categorically that no one except God Almighty can create things from nothing, and only God is capable of reviving people from the dead. Therefore, these verses mean that Jesus[as] would inspire his followers to embrace the path of God to such a degree that it would be as if they had received a new life. The people who would believe in him would be spiritually revived. Earthly people would be transformed to heavenly people and would soar high in the spiritual sky like birds.

According to Islamic teachings miracles are extraordinary events in the sense that no human being, without divine help, can produce them, but they are not against the laws of nature. It is also said that Jesus[as] healed some sick, blind, and deaf people and some lepers by the touch of his hands. It may have been so in some cases, but he certainly restored the sight of the people who were spiritually blind, gave hearing to those who were spiritually deaf, and healed those who were spiritually sick.

The Bible, too, mentions some miracles. It is said that on one occasion there were five thousand people with Jesus[as] and there was very little food for them to eat. Jesus[as] fed them on five loaves and two fish.

On another occasion there were four thousand people: 'Jesus asked his disciples,

"How much bread have you?"

"Seven loaves and a few small fish", they answered.

So Jesus ordered the crowd to sit down on the ground. Then he took the seven loaves and the fish, gave thanks to God, broke them, and gave them to the disciples; and the disciples gave them to the people. They all ate and had enough. Then the disciples took up seven baskets full of pieces left over. The number of men who ate was four thousand, not counting the women and children.'[1]

The number seems to be exaggerated because it is very strange that after witnessing such a great miracle, the people present did not accept him and become his disciples.

Miracles of no less wonder were bestowed upon earlier Prophets of Israel, and even on persons of lower spiritual status. For example, Samson is described in the Bible to have performed impossible deeds under divine inspiration. It is related that when the Philistines attacked the town of Lehi, the men of Judah asked them, 'Why are you attacking us'? They answered, 'We came to take Samson prisoner and to treat him as he treated us.' So three thousand men of Judah went to the cave in the cliff at Etam and said to Samson, 'Don't you know that the Philistines are our rulers? What have you done to us?' He answered, 'I did to them just what they did to me.'

They said, 'We have come here to tie you up, so that we can hand you over to them.' Samson said, 'Give me your word that you won't kill me yourselves.' 'All right', they said, 'we are only going to tie you up and hand you over to them. We won't kill you.' So they tied him up with two new ropes and brought him back from the cave.

When he got to Lehi, the Philistines came running towards him, shouting at him. Suddenly the power of the Lord made him strong and he broke the ropes round his arms and hands as if they

---

1. Matthew 15:34–38

were burnt threads. Then he found the jawbone of a donkey that had recently died. He bent down and picked it up and killed a thousand men with it. So Samson sang:

> *With the jawbone of a donkey*
> *I killed a thousand men;*
> *With the jawbone of a donkey*
> *I piled them up in piles.*[1]

Again, it is related that Samson became very thirsty, so he called to the Lord and said:

> You gave me this great victory; am I now going to die of thirst and be captured by these heathen Philistines? Then God opened a hollow place in the ground there at Lehi, and water came out of it. Samson drank it and began to feel much better.[2]

There are numerous stories in the Bible telling us the miracles performed by different people. How far they can be taken as true happenings, one cannot say.

Christians today emphasise that Jesus[as] being born without the agency of a father is a great miracle and he should be regarded as Divine. No doubt it was a great miracle but the Bible mentions even greater miracles. For example, it is related:

---

1. Judges 15:10–16
2. Judges 15:18–19

> For this Melchizedek, the king of Salem, priest of the Most High God... He is without father, without mother, without descent, having neither beginning of days nor end of life, but resembling the son of God he continues a priest forever.[1]

However unbelievable this is, if Jesus[as] is deemed to be God on the premise that he was born without a father, then why isn't the King of Salem deemed to be a higher God on the premise that he was born without both, father and mother? The fact is that Jesus[as] did not claim to be God or the son of God, instead he claimed to be a true Messenger of God, a Prophet to the Israelites.

Study Questions

QUESTION 1: One of the miracles described in the Holy Quran is that Jesus[as] created some birds. How would you explain this?

YOUR RESPONSE: _____
_____
_____
_____
_____
_____

---

1. Hebrews 7:1–3

QUESTION 2: If a Christian says to you that Jesus[as] was God because he was born without the agency of a father, what arguments would you put forward to prove that he still cannot be God?

YOUR RESPONSE:

Chapter Seven— Enemies Plan to Kill Jesus

The history of religion tells us that whenever God sent His Messengers to this world, the majority of people opposed them and tried to put an end to their message. Jesus[as] was no exception. His message was entirely based on peace and love, yet the Jewish clergy of his time were threatened by the spiritual revolution brought by Jesus[as]. They realised that his teachings were a direct challenge to their own leadership. They were desperate to do something to save their leadership as they feared that it was going to be replaced by the leader appointed by God. They were thus greatly annoyed and wanted to get rid of Jesus[as].

They accused him of changing the accepted religious practices and said that his teachings were leading people astray.

Moreover, they were enraged as he often rebuked them for their hypocrisy and the absurd practices and ceremonies to which they had become accustomed. Jesus[as] told people:

Be on your guard against the teachers of the Law, who like to walk about in their long robes and love to be greeted with respect in the marketplace; who choose the reserved seats in the synagogues and the best places at feasts; who take advantage of widows and rob them of their homes, and then make a show of saying long prayers! Their punishment will be all the worse.[1]

The Jewish clergy, therefore, turned against Jesus[as]. They were determined to put an end to his message and bring about his ruin.

Jesus[as] in Jerusalem

We now take up the story of the arrest of Jesus[as], his subsequent trial and orders of crucifixion by Pontius Pilate, his survival from the cross and meeting his disciples, as mentioned in the Bible.

As the Passover festival was drawing near, large numbers of Jews began preparations to visit Jerusalem to commemorate the delivery of the Israelites from slavery in Egypt many hundreds of years earlier. This is an important Jewish festival. The Orthodox Jews abstain from eating leavened bread during the festival. Instead they use unleavened bread usually in the form of matzoth.

By eating matzoth they recall the unleavened bread eaten by the Israelites during their flight because they had no time to prepare raised bread. During Passover, meals are also prepared and

---

1. Luke 20:46–47

served using sets of utensils and dishes reserved strictly for the festival.

It is said that Jesus[as] went to Jerusalem on this occasion. He rode a donkey provided by his disciples and entered Jerusalem. The crowd greeted him, listened to him, and was very impressed by what he had to say.

The Bible tells us that when Jesus[as] entered Jerusalem, the whole city was thrown into an uproar. 'Who is he?' the people asked. 'This is the Prophet Jesus from Nazareth in Galilee,' the crowds answered.[1]

The chief priests and the teachers of the Law heard the reports of his growing influence and became very worried. It is possible that they had persuaded the authorities to arrest Jesus[as] while he was in Jerusalem. The chief priests and the elders met together in the palace of Caiaphas, the High Priest and made plans to arrest Jesus[as] secretly and put him to death. 'We must not do it during the festival', they said, 'or the people will riot.'[2]

Jesus[as] was aware of their plans. He took necessary precautions but remained in Jerusalem and continued delivering the message of God to the people. One day he and his disciples had their meals together secretly at the home of one of his disciples. When the feast was over they moved hurriedly through the narrow streets towards the city gate. They wanted to be away from the city in order to avoid being arrested. As they came out of the city, they headed towards Gethsemane, a garden on the slope of the Mount of Olives, a hill on the east side of Jerusalem, opposite the Temple.

---

1. Matthew 21:10–11
2. Matthew 26:3–5

Jesus[as] Prays in Gethsemane

When they arrived at Gethsemane, Jesus[as] went off from them about the distance of a stone's throw and knelt down and prayed, 'Father,' he said, 'if You will take this cup of suffering away from me. Not my will, however, but Your will be done.' An angel from heaven appeared to him and strengthened him. In great anguish he prayed even more fervently; his sweat was like drops of blood falling to the ground. Rising from his prayer, he went back to the disciples and found them asleep, worn out by their grief. He said to them, 'Why are you sleeping? Get up and pray that you will not fall into temptation.'[1]

'Once more Jesus went away and prayed, "My Father, if this cup of suffering cannot be taken away unless I drink it, Your will be done." He returned once more and found the disciples asleep; they could not keep their eyes open. Again Jesus left them, went away and prayed the third time, saying the same words. Then he returned to the disciples and said, "Are you still sleeping and resting? Look! The hour has come for the son of man to be handed over to the power of sinful men."'[2]

It is said that Judas, a companion of Jesus[as] betrayed him and led the soldiers to Gethsemane: 'Judas, the traitor, knew where it was, because many times Jesus had met there with his disciples. So Judas went to the garden, taking with him a group of Roman

---

1. Luke 22:41–46
2. Matthew 26:42–45

Jerusalem in New Testament Times

soldiers, and some temple guards sent by the chief priests and the Pharisees; they were armed and carried lanterns and torches.'[1]

Jesus[as] is Arrested

The Roman soldiers with their commanding officer and the Jewish guards arrested Jesus[as], bound him, and took him first to Annas. He was the father-in-law of Caiaphas, who was high priest that year.[2] He questioned him in his own way. Then Annas sent him, still bound, to Caiaphas the high priest.[3] Annas had no official position but he was a former high priest and a leading Sadducee. He was obviously a man of great influence. Perhaps this trial was an informal investigation held to formulate proper charges.[4]

The chief priests and the whole council tried to find some false evidence against Jesus[as] to put him to death; but they could not find any, even though many people came forward and lied about him.[5] Finally, the council condemned Jesus[as] to death on religious grounds of blasphemy. Under Roman rule, however, it was necessary to obtain confirmation of this sentence and its execution from Pilate.

A death sentence passed on Jesus[as] under Jewish law by a

---

1. John 18:2–3
2. John 18:12–13
3. John 18:24
4. *An Introduction to the Bible,* by John Drane p.413; publishing PLC Oxford 1990, published by Lion
5. Matthew 26:59–60

religious court would certainly have influenced the ordinary people against him and it might even have been expected to exert a certain moral pressure on the Roman judge who was to have the final word.[1] The men who were guarding Jesus[as] mocked him and beat him. They blindfolded him and asked him, 'Who hit you? Guess!' And they said many other insulting things to him.[2]

Study Questions

QUESTION 1: Why did the Jews plan to kill Jesus[as]?

YOUR RESPONSE: _____

---

1. *An Introduction to the Bible by John Drane,* p. 424, publishing PLC. Oxford 1990
2. Luke 22:63–65

QUESTION 2: Where was Jesus^{as} arrested?

YOUR RESPONSE: _____

_____

QUESTION 3: Which disciple, according to the Bible, betrayed Jesus^{as}?

YOUR RESPONSE: _____

_____

QUESTION 4: What was the prayer of Jesus^{as} at that critical moment?

YOUR RESPONSE: _____

_____
_____
_____
_____
_____
_____
_____
_____
_____
_____
_____
_____

Chapter Eight—
Trial of Jesus

Early in the morning, all the chief priests and elders made their plans against Jesus[as] to put him to death. They put him in chains, led him off, and handed him over to Pilate, the Roman governor.[1]

They told him that Jesus[as] had committed an act of blasphemy against God. Moreover, they accused him of changing the accepted religious practices and said that his teachings were leading people astray. It appears from these statements that the Jewish religious leaders of that time believed that the punishment prescribed for blasphemy was death, that is why they pleaded with Pilate to put Jesus[as] to death. Strangely, some of the Muslim clergy of today also believe that the punishment for blasphemy should be death. The Government of Pakistan, influenced by the mullahs, has enacted a law which prescribes the only punishment for such a crime as death. It seems therefore that the Muslim clergy

---

1. Matthew 27:1–2

of today ignore the teachings of the Holy Quran which does not mention any such punishment, instead they seem to follow the Jewish laws.

When Pilate heard the charges against Jesus[as] he said to them, 'Then you yourselves take him and try him according to your own law.' They replied, 'We are not allowed to put anyone to death.'[1] They continued to accuse Jesus[as], 'We caught this man misleading our people telling them not to pay taxes to the Emperor and claiming that he himself is the Messiah, a king.' Pilate asked him. 'Are you the king of the Jews?' 'So you say', answered Jesus[as].[2]

Jesus[as] said, 'My kingdom does not belong to this world; if my kingdom belonged to this world, my followers would fight to keep me from being handed over to the Jewish authorities. No, my kingdom does not belong here.'[3] Then Pilate said to the chief priests and the crowd, 'I find no reason to condemn this man.' But they insisted even more strongly, 'With his teaching he is starting a riot among the people all through Judaea. He began in Galilee and now has come here.'

When Pilate heard this, he asked, 'Is this man a Galilean?' When he learnt that Jesus[as] was from the Galilee region ruled by Herod, he sent him to Herod, who was also in Jerusalem at that time. Herod asked Jesus[as] many questions, but Jesus[as] made no answer. The chief priests and the teachers of the Law stepped forward and made strong accusations against Jesus[as]. Herod and his

---

1. John 18:31
2. Luke 23:2, 3
3. John 18:36

soldiers mocked Jesus[as] and treated him with contempt; then they put a fine robe on him and sent him back to Pilate.[1]

Pontius Pilate was convinced beyond any doubt that Jesus[as] was innocent; therefore, he tried to set him free but the Jews protested violently. Pilate called together the chief priests, the leaders, and the people and said to them, 'You brought this man to me and said that he was misleading the people. Now, I have examined him here in your presence, and I have not found him guilty of any of the crimes you accuse him of. Nor did Herod find him guilty for he sent him back to us. There is nothing this man has done to deserve death. So I will have him whipped and let him go'.[2]

However, the Jews insisted that he was a traitor and, therefore, should be hanged. The governor looked at the multitudes of the Jews standing around and when he saw many of the Jews weeping, he said, 'Not all the multitude wishes him to die.' But the elders of the Jews said, 'For this purpose has the whole multitude of us come, that he should die.'[3]

They put so much pressure on Pilate that he could not set Jesus[as] free though he was still anxious to save his life. During the trial, Pilate's wife, who had seen a vision concerning the innocence of Jesus[as], sent a message to him, saying, 'Have nothing to do with that innocent man, because in a dream last night I suffered much on account of him.'[4] At this Pilate made a further attempt to persuade the Jews to agree that Jesus[as] should be released. He gave the

---

1. Luke 23:4–7 and 9–11
2. Luke 23:13–16
3. *Gospel of Nicodemus;* Acts of Pilate, p. 510 by Felix Schcidwcilcr
4. Matthew 27:19

enraged crowd an option either to save the life of Jesus[as] or a notorious criminal named Barabbas. The Bible tells us that at every Passover Festival the Roman governor was in the habit of setting free any one prisoner the crowd asked for. At that time there was a well-known prisoner named Jesus Barabbas. So when the crowd gathered, Pilate asked them, 'Which one do you want me to set free for you? Jesus Barabbas or Jesus called the Messiah'?'[1]

They answered 'Barabbas' because the chief priests and the elders had persuaded the crowd to ask Pilate to set Barabbas free and have Jesus[as] put to death. When Pilate asked them, 'What crime has he committed?' They started shouting at the top of their voices, 'Crucify him.'[2] They even threatened to write to Caesar that Pilate had set free a person who claimed to be a king which meant that Pilate himself was also a rebel against the emperor.

When Pilate saw that it was no use to go on, and a riot might break out, he took some water, washed his hands in front of the crowd, and said, 'I am not responsible for the death of this man! This is your doing.' The whole crowd answered, 'Let the punishment for his death fall on us and our children!'[3]

As a result, Pilate passed the sentence on Jesus[as] that they were asking for. He set free the man they wanted, the one who had been put in prison for riot and murder.[4] This act on the part of Pilate amounts to a confession that Jesus[as] was indeed innocent and that the cruel judgement passed by him was under duress. It is quite

---

1. Matthew 27:15-17
2. Matthew 27:23
3. Matthew 27:24, 25
4. Luke 23:24, 25

clear from the Biblical account that the Jewish community had colluded against Jesus[as] and was determined to have him punished. So a decision by Pilate contrary to the wishes of Jewish clergy would have resulted in a riot.

Friday afternoon was fixed for the crucifixion. Jesus[as] prayed: 'Father, my Father! All things are possible for you. Take this cup of suffering away from me.' He prayed fervently because the truth of his claim was at stake. Jesus[as] knew that if the Jews succeeded in their attempt to kill him by crucifixion, they would proclaim him to be an impostor whose falsehood had finally been proved on the authority of divine scripture, which states, 'A hanged man is accursed by God.'[1]

God's Promise to Save Jesus[as] from the Accursed Death

The prayers of Jesus[as] were accepted and God assured him that he would be saved from the accursed death on the cross. According to the Holy Quran, God said to him, 'I will cause thee to die a natural death and will exalt thee to Myself, and shall clear thee of the charges of those who disbelieve.'[2]

The Bible seems to give a similar message. When the Jews demanded a sign from Jesus[as], he replied, 'A wicked and adulterous generation asks for a miraculous sign; But none will be given to it except the sign of the Prophet Jonah. For as Jonah was three

---

1. Deuteronomy 21:23
2. Holy Quran 3:56

days and three nights in the belly of a huge fish, so the son of man will be three days and three nights in the heart of the earth.'[1]

It is interesting to note that the story of Jonah[as] was also told in the Holy Quran but it does not mention that he remained in the belly of the fish for three days and three nights. The Holy Quran says:

> Surely Jonah was one of the Messengers of Allah. When he fled to the laden ship; And he cast lots with the crew of the ship and was of the losers. And the fish swallowed him while he was blaming himself. And had he not been of those who glorify God, he would have surely remained in its belly till the Day of Resurrection. Then We cast him on a bare tract of land, and he was sick.[2]

Study Questions

QUESTION 1: To which court was Jesus[as] brought for trial?

YOUR RESPONSE: _____
_____
_____

---

1. Matthew 12:39–40
2. Holy Quran 37:140–146

QUESTION 2: What charges were brought against Jesus[as] by the Jews?

YOUR RESPONSE: _____

_____
_____
_____
_____
_____
_____
_____

QUESTION 3: What dream did Pilate's wife have regarding Jesus[as]?

YOUR RESPONSE: _____

_____
_____
_____
_____
_____
_____
_____

QUESTION 4 Who was set free by Pilate on the occasion of Passover?

YOUR RESPONSE: _____

_____
_____

QUESTION 5: Mention a Quranic verse which shows that Jesus[as] did not die on the cross.

YOUR RESPONSE:

QUESTION 6: When the Jews demanded a sign, which sign did Jesus[as] mention to them?

YOUR RESPONSE:

Chapter Nine—
Jesus is Hung on the Cross

On Friday morning, the day fixed for the crucifixion, there was a huge commotion in the city. Most of the enemies of Jesus[as] were looking forward to see him humiliated and disgraced publicly. According to the Bible a crown of thorny branches was put on his head and he was beaten and spat upon. Jesus[as] was taken to Golgotha, the place of execution, about 600 metres away. A great crowd followed him through the streets, jeering at him and hurling insults at him. The Gospel of John tells us that he carried his own cross.

According to a Jewish custom, which was fully endorsed by the Roman law, nobody was permitted to remain on the cross on the Sabbath. The Sabbath begins at sunset on Friday and remains through sunset on Saturday.

In those days the hands and feet of the condemned persons were nailed to the wooden cross, and no food was served to them, so they used to die of hunger and thirst. Death was the result of a slow process which sometimes took three or four days. It was also a practice that the soldiers would break the leg bones of the victims to ensure their death.

The cross was put up on the hill of Golgotha, outside the city wall of Jerusalem. A crowd had gathered there to witness the scene. Mary, the mother of Jesus[as], some disciples, and well-wishers of Jesus[as] were also present. People, passing by, shook their heads and hurled insults at Jesus[as].[1] In the same way the chief priests and the teachers of the Law and the elders jeered at him: 'He saved others but he cannot save himself! Isn't he the king of Israel? If he comes down off the cross now, we will believe in him!'[2] Even the bandits who had been crucified with him insulted him in the same way.[3] Jesus[as] prayed to God and said, 'Forgive them, Father! They don't know what they are doing.'[4]

As related in the Bible, soon after Jesus[as] was put on the cross, the whole country was covered with darkness which lasted for three hours. After remaining for a few hours on the cross Jesus[as] cried in anguish, *Eli, Eli, lama sabachthani?* which means, 'My God, My God, why have You forsaken me?'[5]

Then he said 'I thirst.' A bowl full of vinegar stood there; so they put a sponge full of the vinegar on hyssop and held it to his mouth.[6] Soon after his head drooped and he seemed to have gone

---

1. Matthew 27:39
2. Matthew 27:41-42
3. Matthew 27:44
4. Luke 23:34
5. Matthew 27:46
6. John 19:28, 29

into a coma. 'Jesus[as] was in shock and hypotensive, and lost consciousness because of diminished blood supply to the brain. His ashen skin and immobility were mistaken for death and there is no doubt that the bystanders believed he was dead.'[1]

It seemed that an earthquake shook the whole city at that moment. The Bible states: 'The earth shook and the rocks were split.'[2] The people were terrified and took to their heals.

As the Sabbath was approaching, the soldiers broke the legs of the two bandits. They were alive. They died when their legs were broken, but when they came to Jesus[as], they thought that he had already died. However, one of the soldiers pierced his side with a spear and at once blood and water flowed forth.[3] Surprisingly, the legs of Jesus[as] were not broken.

The rushing of blood and water from his body was a proof that Jesus[as] was alive at that moment and not dead, as medical science tells us that blood and water cannot flow forth from a dead body. If he was dead and his heart had stopped beating, such active bleeding as causing the blood to flow out would be impossible.

Jesus[as] is Saved

One of the followers of Jesus[as] who had not yet become his disciple openly, but believed in him at heart, was Joseph of Arimathea.

---

1. *Journal of the Royal College of Physicians of London;* vol. 25 No.2 April 1991. Article by Trevor. A. Lloyd Davies p. 168.
2. Matthew 27:51
3. John 19:34

He was a rich and influential man and was very close to Pilate. The body of Jesus[as] was handed over to him.

The Bible tells us that Joseph of Arimathea, a respected member of the council, who was also himself looking for the kingdom of God, took courage and went to Pilate and asked for the body of Jesus[as]. Pilate wondered if he were already dead and summoning the centurion, he asked him whether he was already dead. And when he learned from the centurion that he was dead, he granted the body to Joseph.[1]

Thus, under Joseph's supervision the disciples removed the body, wrapped it in a linen shroud, and placed it in a tomb which had been dug out of solid rock. Then they rolled a large stone across the entrance to the tomb. The tomb was spacious enough to accommodate Jesus[as] and one or two attendants to sit and take care of him. It appears that only a few close disciples knew that Jesus[as] was alive. The rest of his disciples, like everybody else, were under the impression that he died on the cross. The Bible mentions coming and going of these disciples to the tomb but everything was done with great caution and in secrecy.

The Bible tells us that the women who had come with Jesus[as] from Galilee followed, and saw the tomb, and how his body was laid; then they returned and prepared spices and ointments.[2] It also tells us that Nicodemus, another follower of Jesus[as], and a man of great repute, 'who at first had gone to see Jesus at night, went

---

1. Mark 15:42–45
2. Luke 23:55, 56

with Joseph taking with him about thirty kilograms of spices, a mixture of myrrh and aloes.'[1]

In fact, the ointment which had been prepared in advance was applied to his wounds. All the ingredients of this ointment have properties of healing wounds and subduing pain. This wonderful ointment known as *Marham-e-Isa,* or the 'Ointment of Jesus', is recorded in many medical books throughout history such as the famous medical treatise known in the West as the 'Canon of Medicine' by Avicenna.[2] This book was used as the standard textbook of medicine in Europe for centuries.

They also smoked the grotto with aloes and other herbs which have tonic qualities to bring Jesus[as] back to consciousness. Thus, 'Jesus lay in the tomb over the Sabbath. He would not regain consciousness for many hours, and in the meantime the spices and linen bandages provided the best dressing for his injuries.'[3] After a short time in the sepulchre, Jesus[as] had recovered sufficiently to be able to walk.

Jews Set a Watch at the Tomb

The Jews themselves were not sure of the death of Jesus[as]. They remembered the prophecy that Jesus[as] had made that he would show them the miracle of Jonah[as] and would come out of the heart

---

1. John 19:39
2. *Al-Qanoon fit-Tibb,* by Ibn Sina, vol. 3, p. 133
3. *The Passover Plot,* by Hugh J. Schonfield, p. 170, published by Macdonald and Jane's London 1974

of the earth alive. Therefore, the chief priest and the Pharisees went again to Pilate and said to him, 'Your Excellency, we recall how that impostor said, that he would rise again after three days. Will you give orders for the sepulchre to be guarded until the third day?'[1] 'Take a guard', Pilate told them, 'go and make the tomb as secure as you can.' So they went and made the sepulchre secure by sealing the stone and leaving the guard on watch.[2]

Jesus[as] Escapes and Meets his Disciples

In spite of the watch and despite the sealing of the tomb, Jesus[as] left the sepulchre before the third day had dawned. As related in the Gospel of Matthew, there seemed to be another violent earthquake which might have rolled the stone away. 'The guards were so afraid that they trembled and became like dead men.'[3]

Very early on the first day of the week, Mary Magdalene and Mary the mother of James, and Salome went to the tomb when the sun had risen. They said to one another, 'Who will roll away the stone for us from the door of the tomb?' Looking up, they saw that the stone was rolled back; it was very large.[4]

Entering the tomb, they saw a young man sitting on the right side dressed in a white robe and they were amazed. He told them,

---

1. Matthew 27:63–64
2. Matthew 27:65–66
3. Matthew 28:4
4. Mark 16:2–4

'He is going to Galilee ahead of you; there you will see him, just as he told you.'[1]

After leaving the sepulchre Jesus[as] is known to have been seen by many of his disciples at different times. Even when some of his disciples were taken by surprise and disbelief, Jesus[as] proved to them that he was the same person who was put on the cross and not a ghost. He seemed to have been moving away from Jerusalem in the direction of Galilee. He avoided public contact intentionally. As he set upon his journey, he met two disciples who were going to a village named Emmaus, about eleven kilometres from Jerusalem. They did not recognise him at first. As they came near the village to which they were going, Jesus[as] acted as if he were going farther.[2] He did not want to go into the village for fear of being recognised.

On another occasion he met some disciples. They were terrified, thinking that they were seeing a ghost. But he said to them, 'Why are you alarmed? Why are these doubts coming up in your minds? Look at my hands and my feet and see that it is I myself. Feel me, and you will know, for a ghost does not have flesh and bones, as you can see I have.' He said this and showed them his hands and his feet. Then he asked them, 'Have you anything here to eat?' They gave him a piece of cooked fish, which he took and ate in their presence.'[3] In this way Jesus[as] proved to them that he was the same person and not a ghost.

The Bible also tells us that when Thomas, one of his disciples,

---

1. Mark 16:7
2. Luke 24:28
3. Luke 24:37–43

learnt that Jesus[as] was alive and well, he said, 'Unless I see the scars of the nails in his hands and put my finger on those scars and my hand in his side I will not believe.'[1] So when he met Jesus[as] along with other disciples, Jesus[as] showed him where the nails were and told Thomas to thrust his finger into the place where the nails were, and into his side to see for himself that he was alive with the same body and not a ghost.

Thus, the prophecy that Jesus[as] made was proved to the letter. Just as Jonah[as] entered the whale's body alive, remained in it alive, though unconscious, and came out of it alive, so Jesus[as] entered the tomb alive, remained there alive, though unconscious, and came out alive. The two incidents mirror each other.

Study Questions

QUESTION 1: Where was the cross set up?

YOUR RESPONSE: _____

_____

_____

_____

_____

_____

_____

---

1. John 20:25

QUESTION 2: What is meant by the statement *Eli Eli Lama Sabachthani*?

YOUR RESPONSE:

QUESTION 3: Why did people think that Jesus[as] was dead?

YOUR RESPONSE:

QUESTION 4: How long did Jesus[as] remain on the cross?

YOUR RESPONSE:

QUESTION 5: How can you prove that Jesus[as] was alive but unconscious when taken down from the cross?

YOUR RESPONSE:

QUESTION 6: Who was Joseph of Arimathea? Where did he take the body of Jesus[as]?

YOUR RESPONSE:

CHAPTER NINE—JESUS IS HUNG ON THE CROSS

QUESTION 7: How long did Jesus^{as} remain in the tomb?

YOUR RESPONSE:

QUESTION 8: Where did Jesus^{as} go after he recovered from his wounds?

YOUR RESPONSE:

QUESTION 9: Why did the disciples think that Jesus^{as} was a ghost?

YOUR RESPONSE:

QUESTION 10: How did Jesus[as] remove their fears and prove to them that he was not a ghost?

YOUR RESPONSE:

QUESTION 11: Jesus[as] prophesied that he would come out alive from the heart of the earth just as Prophet Jonah[as] came out alive from the belly of the whale. Explain how this prophecy was fulfilled?

YOUR RESPONSE:

Chapter Ten—
Chronology of Jesus' Trial

The events leading up to and of the trial of Jesus[as] are of great importance, but they are not easy to ascertain.

'The Gospels appear to report two different trials of Jesus. One was before the Jewish authorities, when he was charged with a religious offence. The other was before the Roman prefect Pontius Pilate, where he was charged with a political offence. Probably the Jews had no authority to carry out a death sentence themselves, and this was why they needed the support of the Roman prefect

It certainly makes good sense to suppose that Jesus' enemies would make much of the charge of blasphemy before a Jewish court and then change to a charge of political revolt as the one most likely to secure the death sentence from a Roman official.'[1]

'In Mark, and Matthew who probably used him, Jesus is arrested by a group of unspecified status which is organised by the

---

1. *An Introduction to the Bible,* by John Drane, p. 413

high priest. He refers to this band as if they were a home guard sent out to catch a bandit by the local authority of a city. He is brought to the high priest and accused by witnesses before the 'chief priests and all the council'. The witnesses cannot agree, Jesus tells the high priest that he is the Messiah and that the 'son of man' will soon be seen coming in clouds of glory; the high priest exclaims at this blasphemy and the meeting adjudges him fit to die. A second meeting in the morning holds a consultation, doubtless as to how to have him killed, and concludes by handing him over to Pilate.'[1]

'Luke's account is subtly different. Jesus is arrested by the Temple police; he is taken to the high priest's house but there is no night time meeting of any council. Only at a morning meeting does a council ask him questions: first, is he Christ? second, is he the 'son of God'? The whole company then brings him to Pilate.'[2]

'In the fourth Gospel events take a very different course... Jesus is never questioned at all before a council of Jews. He is taken first to the house of the high priest's father-in-law Annas, where he is questioned only about his disciples and his teaching. From there he goes to the house of Caiaphas, the high priest, and from there to Pilate's residence.'[3]

According to the Bible it seems that the trials of Jesus[as] before Pilate and possibly before Herod had all happened in the course of Friday morning, which is hard to believe. 'It is difficult to

---

1. *The Unauthorised Version,* by Robin Lane Fox, published by the Penguin Group London Viking in 1991. p. 295
2. *The Unauthorised Version,* by Robin Lane Fox, published by the Penguin Group London Viking in 1991. p. 296
3. *The Unauthorised Version,* by Robin Lane Fox, published by the Penguin Group London Viking in 1991. p. 298

CHAPTER TEN—CHRONOLOGY OF JESUS' TRIAL

imagine that Jesus was brought before Pilate much earlier than six o' clock in the morning when the Jewish day began. Yet within three hours everything is decided and Jesus is at the place of execution. In the interval Pilate had heard the charges against Jesus, has interrogated him, has listened and responded to a plea to release a prisoner according to custom and the people have chosen Barabbas; he has yielded to the demand that Jesus should be crucified, and ordered him to be flogged; the soldiers have taken him away and had their sport with him, and then have led him at a slow pace some distance outside the city to Golgotha. Pilate must surely have condemned Jesus with extraordinary haste, which is not what the other sources convey.

According to Matthew, the wife of Pilate sends to tell him of a dream she has had and begs him not to proceed against Jesus, and so reluctant is the governor to act that he sends for water and publicly washes his hands to signify his guiltlessness. Luke introduces another element of delay. Pilate, learning that Jesus is a Galilean, has him sent to Herod Antipas, in residence at his palace in Jerusalem.'[1]

Moreover, the Biblical account that Jesus[as] was handed over for crucifixion as soon as the trial ended is hard to believe because the preparation for crucifixion could only start after the crucifixion orders. Surely ample time was needed for preparation. Obviously, all these activities cannot possibly fit on a Friday morning.

Again, there is the problem of the Passover Festival which we have to solve in this connection. 'On the particular week that Jesus

---

1. *The Passover Plot,* by Hugh J. Schonfield, published by Macdonald and Jane's, London 1974. p. 128, 129.

was crucified, the Passover was also being celebrated, and this in itself was a special holy day. Putting together this information with what we learn from the Gospels, it seems that the synoptic writers thought that the Friday was the Passover Festival, whereas John believed that the Passover fell on the Sabbath in that particular year.[1] Now if we accept that Friday was the Passover as was told by Mark, Matthew, and Luke, then we cannot envisage the trial, by the Jews or by Pilate, to have happened on a festival day.

'It is most unlikely that Jesus would have been judged, condemned and crucified in the middle of such an important feast as the Passover. In particular, it is unlikely that a Roman governor would have been so foolish as to take the great risk involved in the public execution of a popular figure at a time when Jerusalem was crowded with pilgrims. To have done so would have defiled the day of the great festival, and could easily have sparked off a riot among the Jews. It would have been against Jewish Passover laws for Jesus to be tried in the middle of a festival. All forms of work were prohibited on the Passover, and this includes the work of the Sanhedrin.'[2]

Taking the view of the fourth Gospel into account, which said that Passover was on Saturday, the above objections hold good as all those activities could not have happened in so short a time. It seems that St. John was aware of this problem that no trial could have happened on a festival day, so he tried to resolve it by suggesting that the Passover festival fell on Saturday and not on Friday.

It can be suggested, however, that in order to put Jesus[as] to

---

1. *An Introduction to the Bible,* by John Drane, p. 428
2. *An Introduction to the Bible,* by John Drane, p. 426

death the Jews might have ignored their religious laws. This doesn't seem to be the case as we know that Jews were always keen to follow their religious laws. The fourth Gospel tells us that the Jews did not enter the Roman court for fear of becoming unclean on the eve of Passover. Moreover, 'it is also significant that, of all the charges made by the first Christians against the Jews, they never accused them of breaking the law in order to have Jesus executed.'[1]

It appears from these Biblical accounts that Jesus[as] was arrested on Thursday evening and questioned by the Jewish authorities during the night. According to Mark and Matthew he faced the Jewish Council during the night and again early in the next morning, after which he was taken to Pilate. According to Luke, however, he faced the Jewish Council only in the morning.

Some Christian scholars have disputed this and said that there could not have been a night time meeting of the Jewish Council. One of them says:

> As has been pointed out very convincingly by most Jewish scholars, the historical authenticity of an overnight meeting on this occasion of the full Sanhedrin, the supreme Jewish Council, is extremely doubtful. No normal Sanhedrin meeting ever took place at night and the difficulties of summoning appropriate representatives from their beds at festival time would have been far greater than simply holding Jesus overnight, or indeed over several nights had there been any legitimate trial.[2]

---

1. *An Introduction to the Bible,* by John Drane, p. 425
2. *Jesus, the Evidence,* by Ian Wilson, published by Weidenfeld & Nicolson London 1984, p. 121

The same argument can be put forward for any meeting conducted before daybreak. 'The rabbinic treatise on the Sanhedrin, written c.200 states that its meetings could not be held on a Sabbath or any festival day, let alone by night.'[1] Moreover, 'It has been pointed out, in questioning the accuracy of the account that it would have been unlikely for the Sanhedrin, the supreme Jewish court for dealing with matters relating to the Law to have met in the high priest's house, seeing that it had its own proper place of assembly.'[2] 'Historians have even begun to argue that no such formal Sanhedrin, i.e. night time meeting of the Jewish council, endured in Judea throughout its rule by Herod and his Roman successors.'[3] We, therefore, conclude that no night time meeting of the Sanhedrin was held.

After taking into consideration the sequence of events according to the Bible and the requirements of Jewish Law, it seems unlikely that after the arrest of Jesus[as] on Thursday, the full meeting of the Sanhedrin, comprising seventy one members, could have taken place before Sunday, as Friday was the Passover and Saturday, being the Sabbath, no Jewish trial could have taken place on those days.

Assuming that the Sanhedrin met on Sunday, the verdict of crucifixion could not possibly have been delivered until Monday, following a mandatory 24 hours as required by Jewish Law. Jesus[as] must then have been taken to Pilate for the Roman trial. If Jesus[as]

---

1. *The Unauthorised Version,* p. 289
2. *The Trial of Jesus of Nazareth,* by S.G.F. Brandon, published by Batsford Ltd. London 1968. p. 87
3. *The Unauthorised Version,* p. 291

was also sent to Herod for trial, this may have occupied a further day. It seems, therefore, that Pilate possibly gave orders for crucifixion on Wednesday.

All Gospels agree that Jesus[as] was put on the cross on Friday. It could not have been the Friday immediately after his arrest on Thursday as it was a festival day according to the three Gospels. So it must have been the following Friday. Evidently, the Gospel writers have confused the issue. They thought that Jesus[as] was tried and put on the cross a day after his arrest, while it seems more logical that he was put on the cross on the following Friday, which was not a holy day for the Jews.

By fixing Friday it seems that Pilate was deliberately trying to minimise the time Jesus[as] would be on the cross, as he knew that all bodies have to be taken down from the cross before Friday's sunset, when the Sabbath begins.

In view of all facts discussed above, a possible sequence of events could be as follows:

POSSIBLE SEQUENCE OF EVENTS

	DAY OF THE WEEK	EVENT
1	Thursday	Arrest of Jesus[as]
2	Friday	Passover Festival
3	Saturday	The Sabbath
4	Sunday	Jewish Council Meeting
5	Monday	Verdict of the Jewish Council
6	Tuesday	Trial by Pilate/Herod
7	Wednesday	Trial by Pilate and Verdict of Crucifixion
8	Thursday	Remained in custody
9	Friday	Jesus[as] put on the cross, taken down and placed in a sepulchre
10	Saturday	Remained in custody
11	Sunday	Left the sepulchre in the morning for Galilee

Study Questions

QUESTION 1: What is the Sanhedrin?

YOUR RESPONSE:

QUESTION 2: Why do you think that the meeting of Sanhedrin could not have taken place at night or on a festival day?

YOUR RESPONSE:

QUESTION 3: What does the term 'synoptic writers' mean?

YOUR RESPONSE: _____
_____
_____

QUESTION 4: Which day was mentioned by the 'synoptic writers' as the Passover day?

YOUR RESPONSE: _____

QUESTION 5: Which day was mentioned by the fourth Gospel as Passover Festival day?

YOUR RESPONSE: _____

QUESTION 16 Why did Pilate give orders for Jesus[as] to be crucified on Friday?

YOUR RESPONSE: _____
_____
_____
_____
_____
_____

Chapter Eleven—
Jesus Migrates to Other Countries

In Search of the Lost Sheep

While still in Palestine Jesus[as] had given sufficient indications, though in parables as was his habit, that in the future he would have to leave Palestine for another country.

As he was moving away from Palestine, the question arose, as to where Jesus[as] should go. This has already been answered by Jesus[as] himself; 'I have been sent only to those lost sheep, the people of Israel.'[1]

'I have other sheep, that are not of this fold, I must bring them also, and they will heed my voice. So there shall be one flock and one shepherd.'[2]

Obviously Jesus[as] would now go in search of the lost tribes of

---

1. Matthew 15:24
2. John 10:16

Israel. In order to evade arrest he had to move away from the danger. Both the Jews and the Roman authorities were his enemies. He thus followed the same ancient route which was taken by the Jews during their historic dispersion.

Lost Tribes of Israel

If we glance at the history of Jews, we find that they were divided into twelve tribes. All of them lived peacefully under Hazrat Dawood[as] (David) and after his death under Hazrat Sulaimaan[as] (Solomon) who were both prophets of God as well as their kings. According to the Bible, their kingdom included all the nations from the river Euphrates to as far west as the city of Gaza in Philistia and the Egyptian border. After the death of King Solomon in 931 BC, his son Rehoboam succeeded him as king. He was very cruel so the people rebelled against him and his kingdom was reduced to the territory of Judah. Jerusalem was the capital of this southern kingdom. Only two tribes, Judah and Benjamin remained loyal to Rehoboam. The remaining ten tribes formed the northern kingdom of Israel, with its capital at SAMARIA and made Jeroboam as their king. There was continual warfare between the two kingdoms.

Jeroboam, according to the Bible, was an official in Solomon's kingdom. He revolted against King Solomon and in order to avoid his wrath escaped to Egypt and stayed there until Solomon's death. About two hundred years later Assyrians under king Tiglath Pilser III (745–727 BC.) attacked the northern kingdom of Israel and captured many cities and took their people to Assyria

CHAPTER ELEVEN—JESUS MIGRATES TO OTHER COUNTRIES

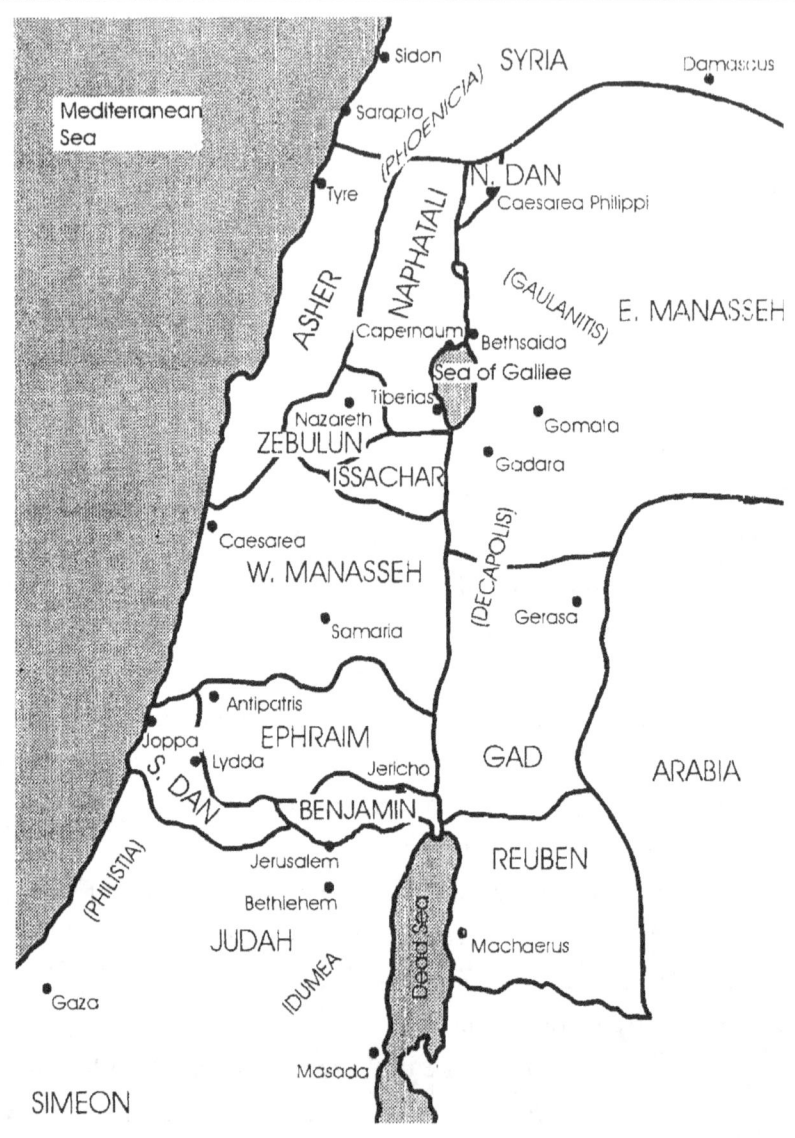

The 12 tribal territories

Names of the Tribes

1 Asher	2 Benjamin	3 Dan	4 Ephraim
5 Gad	6 Issachar	7 Judah	8 Manasseh
9 Naphtali	10 Reuben	11 Simeon	12 Zebulun

as prisoners. Thus began the captivity and dispersion of the ten tribes.

A few years later emperor Shalmaneser V of Assyria attacked the kingdom of Israel. King Hoshea of Israel surrendered and agreed to pay him tribute every year. But one year king Hoshea sent messengers to the king of Egypt asking for his help and stopped paying the annual tribute to Assyria. When Shalmaneser learnt this, he reacted very strongly, invaded Israel and besieged Samaria, which lasted for three years. During this time emperor Shalmaneser died. His successor Sargon II continued the attack, and in 722 BC destroyed the kingdom completely and carried almost all the remainder of the ten tribes to Assyria, Mesopotamia and parts of Media. Henceforth, these ten tribes were known as the Lost Tribes. Further dispersion of the ten tribes took place when the Babylonians destroyed the Assyrians.

Later, the Persians under King Cyrus crushed the Babylonian Empire in 539 BC. The Israelites thus suffered again and were scattered throughout the Persian Empire which at that time extended up to Afghanistan and India. These were the lost tribes of Israel that Jesus[as] went in search of.

Jesus[as] Travels to the East

It appears that Jesus[as] left Galilee and followed the caravan route to Syria, where there was a large Jewish community settled in and around Damascus. There are indications that from Damascus Jesus[as] travelled to Nisibain, a city about 450 miles from Jerusalem, which is on the route from Syria to Persia. A well known Persian historical work known as *Rauzat-us-Safaa* describes an account of the travels of Jesus[as] to Nisibain.

It states, 'Jesus, on whom be peace, was named the Messiah as he was a great traveller. With a woollen scarf on his head and woollen cloak on his body, and a stick in his hand, he wandered on foot from country to country and from city to city. He ate wild fruit and vegetation and at night stayed where he happened to be. In one of his travels, his companions bought a horse for him. He rode the horse one day but as he could not make any provision for the feeding of the horse, he returned it.

When he arrived in Nisibain, which was at a distance of several hundred miles from his home, he sent some of his disciples into the city to preach. There were current wrong and unfounded rumours in the city about Jesus and his mother. The governor therefore arrested the disciples and summoned Jesus. Jesus preached to the people, healed some sick persons by his prayers and also showed some other miracles to them; as a result the king of Nisibain, with all his armies and his people became his follower.'[1]

Jesus[as] in Persia

It seems that by going to Nisibain, Jesus[as] intended to travel towards the east to Afghanistan through Persia. During the course of his journey, Jesus[as] passed through Herat, a town in

---

1. *Rauzat-us-Safaa* was written in 836 AH (1417 AD) by Muhammad bin Khawand and reprinted at Bombay in 1271 AH (1852 AD) on pages 130–135.

Afghanistan near the border of Iran. This is evident from a brief account of a community of people who claim to be the followers of Jesus[as] and are found even today, in and around Herat. In the book called *Among the Dervishes*, it is stated:

> 'The followers of Isa, son of Maryam—Jesus, son of Mary, generally call themselves Moslems and inhabit a number of villages scattered throughout the western area of Afghanistan whose centre is Herat. They believe in the doctrine that Jesus was the 'son of God' because he had attained that rank through his goodness and sacrifice. According to these people, Jesus escaped from the cross, was hidden by friends, was helped to flee to India... and settled in Kashmir where he is revered as an ancient teacher, Yuz Asaf. It is from this period of the supposed life of Jesus that these people claim to have got their message.[1]

It appears that after leaving Nisibain, Jesus[as] assumed the name of Yuz Asaf as he was sometimes known by this name in the countries he subsequently visited. *Yuz* is derived from *Yusu* meaning *Jesus,* and *Asaf* means the *gatherer* or *collector.* Thus, *Yuz Asaf* means *Jesus, the Gatherer* of the Lost Sheep of Israel.

---

1. *Among the Dervishes,* by O.M.Burke, published by Octagon Press Ltd. London, p. 107–109.

Jesus[as] in Afghanistan

From Herat Jesus[as] seems to have entered Afghanistan and then through Punjab to Kashmir where the lost tribes of Israel were known to have settled. There are also indications that Jesus[as] might have visited Tibet.

When we study the customs and habits of the inhabitants of those countries, especially Afghanistan and Kashmir, we are surprised to find that the Afghans and the Kashmiris resemble the Israelites greatly and are very dissimilar to the people of the Indian Subcontinent in their habits and complexion. The Afghans, themselves claim that they are the descendants of Israelites and their features certainly support their claim and so do several of the names of their tribes. For example, Musa Khel means the tribe of Moses; Daud Khel, the tribe of David; Yusuf Zai, the tribe of Joseph; and Solaiman Zai, the tribe of Solomon. Similarly, the names of several of their geographical locations appear to have Jewish origin.

Jesus[as] in India

From Afghanistan Jesus[as] most likely travelled through the Punjab in India to finally settle in Kashmir. In Kashmir, most of the Israelites had adopted Buddhism. Some, even had become idol worshippers. Slowly and gradually Jesus[as] brought them back to the true faith and they accepted him as a Prophet of God.

As time passed Jesus[as] had a great following even in Kashmir.

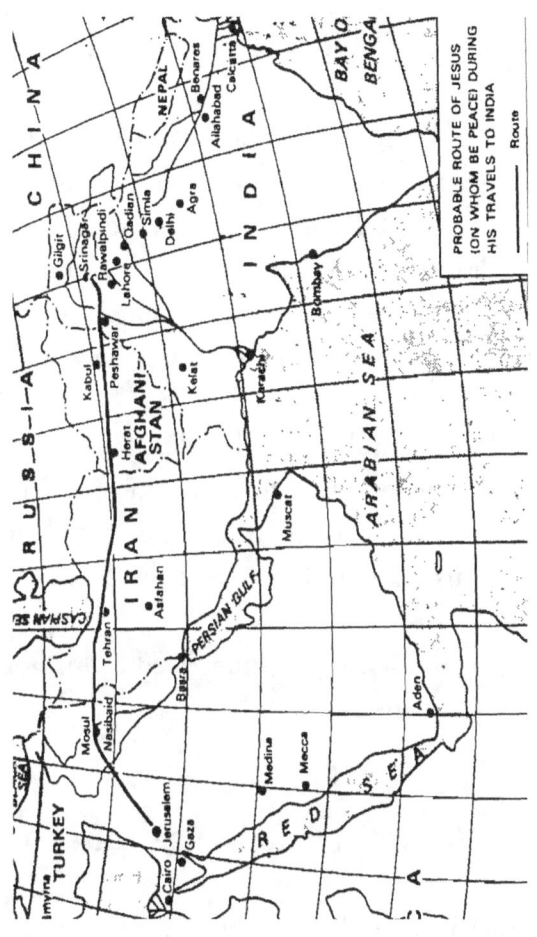

He was held in great honour. Thus, he was accepted in all the lands where the lost tribes of Israel had settled.

Jesus[as] Meets A Hindu King

In a very old Sanskrit book called *Bhavishya Maha Purana*, a meeting between King Shalewahin and Jesus[as] is described. It is reported that once King Shalewahin went to a peak of the Himalayas. There, in the middle of the Hun country the mighty king saw a dignified person of fair complexion wearing white clothes, sitting in the mountain. Shalewahin asked him who he was?

He replied with a smile, 'I am the Messiah, born of a virgin.'

He also told the king that he had come from a far off land where he suffered at the hands of his people. When the king asked him to explain his religion, Jesus[as] replied: 'It is love, truth and purity of heart.'

King Shalewahin was deeply impressed by his holiness, so he left after paying homage to him.[1]

Jesus[as] Dies in Kashmir

Jesus, may peace be upon him, is believed to have died at the age of 120 and was buried in Kashmir. Guided by divine revelation and subsequent research, Hazrat Mirza Ghulam Ahmad[as], the

---

1. *Bhavishya Maha Purana,* written in 3191 Laukika era (115 AD)

Tomb of Jesus in Srinagar, Kashmir, India

Founder of the Ahmadiyya Muslim Community, located his tomb in the Khanyar sector of the city of Srinagar, where it has now become well known and continues to attract thousands of visitors from all parts of the world. The tomb is known as the Tomb of Yuz Asaf. The grave, according to Jewish custom, is east-west in direction, while it is a well-known fact that Muslims, in that part of the world, bury their dead in the north-south direction. The Hindus and the Buddhists, on the other hand, cremate their dead.

This discovery is further of evidence to the fact that Jesus[as] did not die on the cross and that he had travelled to India to accomplish the divine mission, for which he was sent into this world. May his soul rest in peace.

The Holy Quran mentions the place of his final refuge in the following words:

> And we made the son of Mary and his mother a Sign, and gave them shelter on a pleasant plateau with springs of running water.[1]

This is an accurate description of the beautiful valley of Kashmir, where Jesus[as] and his mother finally settled and lived in peace and tranquillity after his escape from Palestine. Kashmir is famous throughout the world for its natural beauty. It is called the 'valley of eternal bliss' and sometimes 'heaven on earth'. Thus this 'heaven on earth' became the place of eternal rest for Jesus[as] and his mother.

It is also believed that Mary died and was buried at a place

---

1. Holy Quran 23:51

called Mari or Murree, named in her honour. Her grave which is known as 'The resting place of mother Mary' can be visited even today. Murree is situated in Northern Pakistan not far from Islamabad, the capital of Pakistan, and is part of the mountainous range which extends into Kashmir.

The Holy Quran tells us in clear terms that Jesus[as] had died. It says:

> The Messiah, son of Mary, was only a Messenger. All Messengers have indeed passed away before him. And his mother was a truthful woman. They both used to eat food.[1]

At another place it says:

> Muhammad is only a Messenger. All Messengers have indeed passed away before him.[2]

---

1. Holy Quran 5:76
2. Holy Quran 3:145

Study Question

QUESTION 1: Who were the 'lost sheep of the house of Israel'? How many tribes did the Jews have?

YOUR RESPONSE: _____

_____
_____
_____
_____
_____
_____

QUESTION 2: Which of the tribes remained loyal to the Southern Kingdom?

YOUR RESPONSE: _____

_____
_____
_____

QUESTION 3: Name the capital of Southern Kingdom.

YOUR RESPONSE: _____

QUESTION 4: Who was the king of this Kingdom?

YOUR RESPONSE: _____

QUESTION 5: Name the capital of the Northern Kingdom?

YOUR RESPONSE: _____

QUESTION 2: Who was the king of the Northern kingdom?

YOUR RESPONSE: _____

QUESTION 6: What was the cause of the division of the Jewish tribes?

YOUR RESPONSE: _____
_____
_____
_____
_____
_____
_____
_____
_____
_____

QUESTION 7: Which Assyrian kings attacked the Northern kingdom and took the people away as prisoners?

YOUR RESPONSE:

QUESTION 8: Which countries did Jesus[as] pass through during his journey to India and why?

YOUR RESPONSE:

QUESTION 9: Who was called 'Yuz Asaf'? What does it mean?

YOUR RESPONSE:

QUESTION 10: How could you tell that the Afghans are the descendants of Israelites?

YOUR RESPONSE:

QUESTION 11: Which book describes a meeting between Raja Shalewahin and Jesus[as]?

YOUR RESPONSE:

QUESTION 12: Who located the tomb of Jesus[as] in Kashmir?

YOUR RESPONSE:

QUESTION 3: How can you refute the non-Ahmadi Muslims' claim that Jesus[as] is physically alive in heaven and will come back to the earth?

YOUR RESPONSE:

Chapter Twelve—
The Shroud of Turin

Millions of people believe that the Shroud of Turin is the very linen cloth in which Jesus[as] was wrapped after he was taken down from the cross. However, there are others who believe that it is fake and therefore challenge its authenticity.

The Shroud is rarely displayed to the public, but when it is, it draws millions of people to the Cathedral of Turin in Italy, where it is kept with utmost security.

Those who believe it to be genuine, point out that it contains a remarkable image of a life size bearded man with long hair. One half of the cloth bears the front image of a man while the other half shows the back. The image bears obvious marks of crucifixion. There are blood streaks which encircle the head probably due to the crown of thorns. Nail wounds also appear on the wrists. One large mark of blood flow is seen on the left side of the chest which corresponds to the piercing of right side of the body. Impressions from the scourging could also be seen on the body. From these blood marks, one can infer that Jesus[as] was alive when wrapped in this cloth.

The cloth is 434 centimetres long and 109 centimetres wide. Scientists have performed many tests on the shroud to see whether it is genuine or not.

In 1978, a team of researchers found that the bloodstains on the cloth appeared to be human blood. The team concluded that the image was probably caused by a human body. Other scientists found that the pollens and limestone dust from the cloth could have come from the region of Palestine. However, the results were not conclusive.

In 1988, scientists used another test called radio carbon dating on the cloth from the shroud in order to determine its age. The results indicated that the shroud dates back to about 1200. The Roman churches accepted the results and declared that the Turin Shroud was fake. However, some historians and scientists have challenged this conclusion. The controversy is far from over.

Moreover, those who regard it as fake and declare that the imprint on the shroud was the work of an artist have never given a satisfactory explanation of the negative image on the cloth. It is difficult enough to reproduce the positive of a picture with such delicate light shading, but to achieve a perfect negative by artificial means is very hard to imagine.

For those who accept it as genuine and regard it as very holy, it furnishes a corroborative evidence in support of the theory that the body of Jesus[as] was removed from the cross while he was still alive.

Study Questions

QUESTION 1: What is the Shroud of Turin?

YOUR RESPONSE:

QUESTION 2: Where is it placed?

YOUR RESPONSE:

QUESTION 3: Supposing that the Turin Shroud is genuine, how would you prove that Jesus[as] was alive when taken down from the cross?

YOUR RESPONSE:

Chapter Thirteen—
The Second Advent of Jesus

Jesus[as] is reported to have said:

> The sun will be darkened, the moon will not give its light, and the stars will fall from heaven, and the celestial powers will be shaken. Then the sign of the son of man will appear in the sky.[1]

This sign appears to refer to the eclipses of the sun and the moon at the time of the second advent of Jesus[as]. The Holy Prophet of Islam, Muhammad[saw], had made a similar prophecy. He indicated a very clear sign of the appearance of the Mahdi, whom Muslims were waiting for.

In *Sunan ad-Daar Qutni,* an eminent and recognised book

---

1. Matthew 24:29–30

Ḥaḍrat Mirza Ghulam Ahmad of Qadian
The Promised Messiah & Mahdi^{as}

on the sayings of the Holy Prophet Muhammad[saw], the following prophecy is recorded:

> For our Mahdi there shall be two signs which have never been manifested before since the creation of the heavens and the earth. In the month of Ramadan, the moon will be eclipsed on the first of its nights [of eclipse], and the sun will be eclipsed on the middle day of its days [of eclipse] and both will occur in the same month of Ramadan. These two signs have never occurred before since Allah created the heavens and the earth.

The eclipse of the moon normally occurs on the 13th, 14th, or 15th night of a lunar month, and the eclipse of the sun on the 27th, 28th, or 29th of the lunar month. The sign mentioned by the Holy Prophet[saw], therefore, was that the moon would be eclipsed on the 13th night of the lunar month and the eclipse of the sun on the 28th of the same lunar month, which will be the month of Ramadan. This sign was to appear after and not before the advent of the Mahdi. He also explained that the Mahdi and the Messiah would be one and the same person. It is reported in one book of traditions, *Ibn Majah:* 'There is no Mahdi except Jesus.'[1]

It so happened that an eclipse of the moon occurred on the 13th of Ramadan, March 21, 1894 and the eclipse of the sun occurred on the 28th of the same month of Ramadan, April 6, 1894, in exact accord with the prophecy of the Holy Prophet Muhammad[saw]. The same phenomenon of double eclipses was repeated in the

---

1. *Sunan Ibn Majah, Baab Shiddatuz-Zamaan*

Western hemisphere in 1895. This was such a magnificent sign that it was impossible for any person to manufacture or improvise.

These prophecies were fulfilled in the lifetime of Hazrat Mirza Ghulam Ahmad[as] of Qadian, India, who claimed to be the Mahdi and the Promised Messiah, and had founded a community in 1889, five years before the appearance of these heavenly signs.

Jesus[as] also foretold the state of the world at the time of his second advent. He said, 'Countries will fight each other, kingdoms will attack one another. There will be famines and earthquakes everywhere.'[1]

All these signs point to the present age when famines, epidemics, plague, and earthquakes are taking place in various parts of the world and the nations are at war with each other. These signs have been manifested which means that the second advent of Jesus[as] had come about in the person of someone who came in the power and spirit of Jesus[as].

The Muslims, too, were looking forward to the advent of the Mahdi and the Messiah. There was general agreement among Muslims that the Mahdi would appear at the beginning of the fourteenth century of the Islamic era. This they inferred from a tradition of the Holy Prophet. That century has elapsed. We find that the only successful claimant to the role of Mahdi and Messiah is Hazrat Mirza Ghulam Ahmad[as] of Qadian, who claimed that the prophecies predicting the appearance of a divinely inspired teacher, in the latter days, had been fulfilled in his person.

Hazrat Mirza Ghulam Ahmad[as] of Qadian wrote a book entitled *Jesus in India* in 1899 in which he declared that Jesus[as] did

---

1. Matthew 24:7

not die on the cross as was claimed by the Jews and the Christians and did not ascend to heaven as is believed by the Christians and majority of Muslims. Jesus[as] was saved from the accursed death on the cross, migrated to the countries where the lost tribes of Israel had settled, and after completing his mission died in Kashmir. The second advent of Jesus[as], therefore, meant that someone else would come in his spirit as no one who has departed from this world had ever returned.

Hazrat Ahmad[as] also declared that God had told him that he is the very Promised Messiah, for whom the Christians and Muslims were waiting for, who had come in the spirit of Jesus[as].

God revealed to Hazrat Ahmad[as]: 'The Messiah, son of Mary, Prophet of God, is dead. It is you who have appeared in his spirit according to the promise. The promise of God is always fulfilled.'[1]

In his Urdu poetry he wrote:

ابن مریم مر گیا حق کی قسم داخل جنت ہوا وہ محترم

God is witness that the son of Mary had died;
That revered one dwells in Paradise.

وقت تھا وقت مسیحا نہ کسی اور کا وقت میں نہ آتا تو کوئی اور ہی آیا ہوتا

The time demanded the advent of the Messiah,
  Not of anyone else;
Had I not come,
  Someone else would have come in my place.

---

1. *Ruhaani Khazaa'in, Izaala-e-Auhaam*, vol. 3, p. 402

Study Questions

QUESTION 1: Which book mentions Holy Prophet's prophecy regarding the advent of the Mahdi?

YOUR RESPONSE:

QUESTION 2: What was the prophecy and how was it fulfilled?

YOUR RESPONSE:

QUESTION 3: Mention the hadith which says that Mahdi and the Messiah would be the same person.

YOUR RESPONSE:

QUESTION 4: Name the book which the Promised Messiah^{as} wrote to remove the doubts over Jesus' death on the cross and his subsequent journey to India.

YOUR RESPONSE: _____

_____
_____
_____
_____
_____

QUESTION 5: What was the name of the Promised Messiah^{as}?

YOUR RESPONSE: _____

_____

Names of Prophets

According to a tradition of the Holy Prophet[saw], the number of Prophets is one hundred and twenty four thousand. Only a small number of these are mentioned by name in the Holy Quran. The Prophets specifically mentioned in the Holy Quran are:

Abraham Hazrat Ibrahim[as]

Adam Hazrat Aadam[as]

Aron Hazrat Haaroon[as]

David Hazrat Dawood[as]

Elijah Hazrat Ilyaas[as]

Elisha Hazrat Al-Yasa'[as]

Enoch Hazrat Idrees[as]

Ezekiel Hazrat Dhul-Kifl[as]

Hud Hazrat Hud[as]

Ishmael Hazrat Ismaa'eel[as]

Isaac Hazrat Is'haaq[as]

Jacob Hazrat Ya'qoob[as]

Jesus Hazrat 'Isa[as]

Jethro Hazrat Shu'aib[as]

Jonah Hazrat Yunus^{as}

Job Hazrat Ayyub^{as}

John the Baptist Hazrat Yahyaa^{as}

Joseph Hazrat Yusuf^{as}

Lot Hazrat Lut^{as}

Muhammad Hazrat Muhammad^{saw}

Moses Hazrat Musa^{as}

Noah Hazrat Nuh^{as}

Saaleh Hazrat Saaleh^{as}

Solomon Hazrat Sulaimaan^{as}

Zechariah Hazrat Zakariyyaa^{as}

Publisher's Note

Salutations are recited out of respect when mentioning the names of Prophets and holy personages. These salutations have been abbreviated and inserted into the text where applicable. Readers are urged to recite the full salutations for the following abbreviations:

saw   *Sallallaahu 'alaihi wa sallam,* meaning 'May peace and blessings of Allah be upon him', is written after the name of the Holy Prophet Muhammad[saw].

as   *Alaihis-salaam/ Alaihas-salaam,* meaning 'May peace be on him/her', is written after the names of Prophets other than the Holy Prophet Muhammad[saw].

ra   *Radiyallaahu 'anhu/'anhaa/'anhum,* meaning 'May Allah be pleased with him/her/them', is written after the names of the Companions of the Holy Prophet Muhammad[saw] or of the Promised Messiah[as].

rta *Rahmatullaah 'alaihi/'alaihaa/'alaihim,* meaning 'May Allah shower His mercy upon him/her/them', is written after the names of those deceased pious Muslims who are not Companions of the Holy Prophet Muhammad[saw] or of the Promised Messiah[as].

Glossary

Abrogate Repeal, Cancel.

Abundance Plenty

Admonition Warning

Agony Extreme physical or mental torture.

Almsgiving Charity, Zakat.

Aloes A sweet smelling liquid produced from a plant.

Anguish: mental suffering.

Bandit Robber, Outlaw.

Benign Kindly

Bestow Give

Blasphemy Saying or doing something that shows disrespect for God and is considered shocking.

Celestial Concerned with sky.

Censure Reprove, Criticise harshly, Reprimand.

Centurion An officer in the Roman army.

Cleave Split into parts violently.

Colluded Agreed secretly.

Concocted Invented.

Covenant Agreement.

Cremate To burn the dead body as part of funeral service.

Decreed Decided.

Dedicated Devoted to a sacred purpose.

Defiled To do something which is offensive to the sacred person or place.

Desist Stop doing it.

Duress Threat.

Exhort To urge, To admonish.

Fore-runner Predecessor

Forsake To withdraw help. Abandon.

Gentile A person who is not a Jew.

Grieve To feel very sad about something that has happened.

Hideous Extremely unpleasant; Ugly.

High Priest The chief Jewish priest and president of Jewish supreme council.

Homage To show respect; To honour.

Hypotensive With low blood pressure.

Hyssop A small bushy plant used in religious ceremonies to sprinkle liquids.

Immune Exempt.

Impostor False claimant to Prophethood

Interpolated Additions to sacred writings.

Leavened Bread Bread made using yeast.

Metaphor Using words not with their ordinary meaning, but trying to describe a situation by using images or symbols.

Mortified Humiliated;

Multitude Crowd of people.

Myrrh A sweet smelling gummy substance produced from the sap of certain trees and shrubs.

Omnipotence Having total power.

Parable A story used to illustrate spiritual lesson, Allegory.

Perplexed Puzzled, Confused;

Pharisees A Jewish religious

group during the time of Jesus[as].

Progeny Children.

Sadducees A small Jewish religious group of old times. Most of them were priests.

Scandulous Outrageous, Shocking.

Secluded Isolated.

Seclusion Away from other people, Isolation.

Sepulchre A tomb cut in rock.

Synonym Word or expression that means the same as another word or expression.

Synoptic The first three Gospel writers, i.e. Mark, Matthew and Luke.

Tidings News.

Traditions Sayings of the Holy Prophet Muhammad, peace and blessings of Allah be upon him.

Unleavened Bread Bread made without using yeast.

Vow Promise to God.

The True Story of Jesus

The True Story of Jesus is a simple yet comprehensive biography of the Prophet Jesus[as], including his miraculous birth, life, death, and second advent. In particular, it features the events preceding his birth, his childhood, his message, and the circumstances surrounding the Crucifixion. It also sheds light upon the Ahmadi Muslim belief of his subsequent migration from Judea, his death in what is now Kashmir, and even his return in the Latter Days as foretold by various noble religious traditions.

While the style and tone is aimed at younger readers, the book presents a scholarly argument with authentic and appropriate references from both the Holy Quran and the Holy Bible. It is a must read for anyone passionate about the true story of Prophet Jesus[as].

www.ingramcontent.com/pod-product-compliance
Lightning Source LLC
LaVergne TN
LVHW011724060526
838200LV00051B/3013